EVERYBODY TAKES TURNS

Dorothy Corey
Pictures by Lois Axeman

Albert Whitman & Company, Chicago

Published simultaneously in Canada
by General Publishing, Limited, Toronto

Library of Congress Cataloging in Publication Data
Corey, Dorothy
Everybody takes turns

(A Self-starter book)
SUMMARY: Brief text and pictures illustrate some of the occasions in life for which we must take our turn.
1. Patience—Juvenile literature. [1. Sharing]
I. Axeman, Lois. II. Title
BJ1533.P3C67 175 79-18652
ISBN 0-8075-2166-3

For Dr. Garnet Larson

I take a turn.

You take a turn.

I have a turn.

You have a turn.

I take a turn first.

You take a turn second.

You have a turn.

I have a turn.

Jim has a turn, too.

I get a turn.

My dog gets a turn.

I get a turn.

You get a turn.

All the children get turns.

Mother tells me
when my turn is up.

Then Tim has a turn.

You take a turn.

I take a turn.

We all take turns.

SANTA

Small children take turns.

Big children take turns.

And grownups take turns
all the time.

People driving and

people walking take turns.

CIRCUS

All kinds of people take turns.

It's fun to have your turn!